INSTRUCTIONS FOR ARMOURERS

Rifles No. 1,
No. 2
and Rifle No. 3 (Pattern 14)

INSTRUCTIONS FOR ARMOURERS
Rifles No. 1, No. 2 and No. 3 (Pattern 14)

ISBN 978-0-934523-11-0 Trade Paperback

Cover Photo:
Short Magazine Lee Enfield Mk I (1903), UK. Caliber .303 British. From the collections of Armémuseum (Swedish Army Museum), Stockholm. Public Domain

Table of Contents

SECTION 1.

Stripping of Rifles No. 1 and No. 2

Re-Assembly of Rifles No. 1 and No. 2

To Strip Rifle No. 3

To Re-assemble Rifle No. 3

SECTION 2.

Cleaning and Lubricating

SECTION 3.

Examination of Rifles No. 1 and No. 2

Rifles No. 3 (Pattern 14)

SECTION 4.

Repairs, Modifications, Adjustments
Rifles No. 1, No. 2

Rifles No. 3 with Telescope sight

Sight
Telescopic
Rifle No. 3 Mark I* (T)

Section 5
Re-Browning - Re-blacking

Section 6
Description and Use of Armourer's
Gauges and Certain Tools

List of Illustrations:

Section 1.
Stripping and Re-assembling

1.   To strip Rifles No. 1 Mark III & III* and No. 2 Mark IV
Remove the nose-cap screws front and back, and nose-cap.
Remove the outer band screw, swivel, outer band, and front
handguard with cap and screws.
Remove the inner band screw and spring.
Remove the magazine.
Remove the screws, guard, front and back.
Remove the guard, trigger pin and trigger.
Raise the back sight leaf, and remove the handguard, rear.

- † Remove the fore-end, with stud and spring, and the
  protector with nut, and screw.

Remove the butt plate screws, butt plate, wad, stock bolt and stock
butt.
Remove the bolt from the body—*see* para. 2.
Remove the locking bolt spring screw, spring, and washer (or
aperture sight), locking bolt, and safety catch.
Remove the sear spring.
Remove the sear screw, retaining spring and sear.
Remove the magazine catch pin and catch.
Remove the cut-off screw, and cut-off (rifles No. 1 Mk III only).
Remove the sight leaf—*see* para. 5.

- *Attention is drawn to the importance of removing the fore-end
before attempting to unscrew the stock bolt.*
† *In No. I, Mk. III, rifles of early manufacture, fitted with long-range
sights, raise the aperture sight and, when necessary, remove the dial sight
screw washer and dial sight before removing the fore-end.*

Key Plate

RIFLE Nº1 S.M.L.E. .303 MK.III
(With Cut-Off)

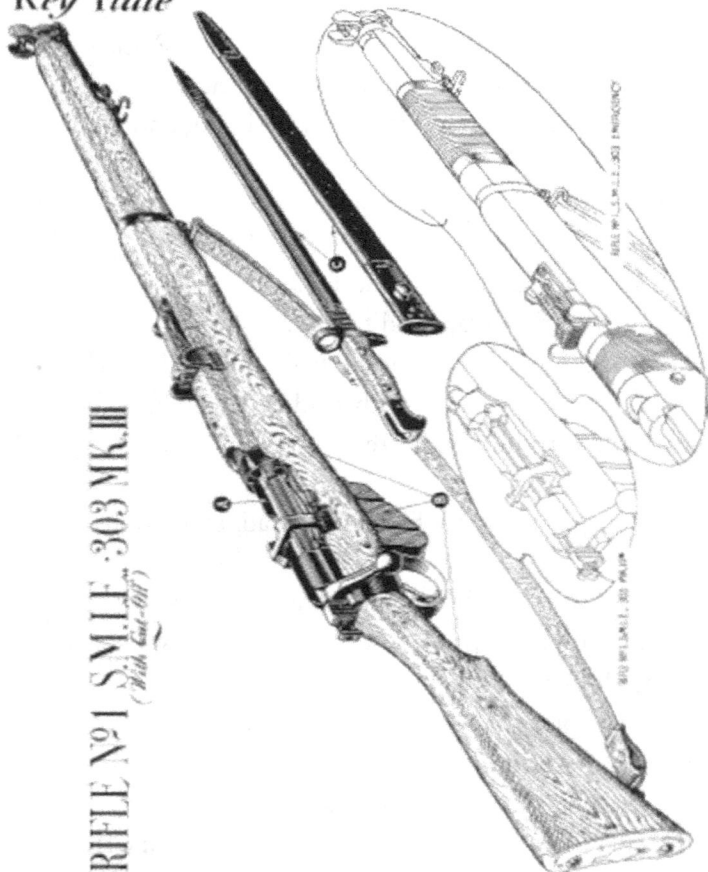

2. *To remove the bolt from the body:*—

Raise the knob with the right hand as far as it will go, draw back the bolt head to the resisting shoulder, release the bolt-head with the forefinger of the right hand from the retaining spring, raise the bolt-head to the full extent, and draw back and remove the bolt.

3. *To strip the bolt of rifles No. 1:—*
Remove the extractor spring, extractor screw and extractor. Remove the striker screw; see that the stud on the cocking-piece is in the short cam; unscrew the bolt-head; unscrew the striker and remove the mainspring.

4. *To strip the bolt of rifles No. 2, Mk. IV*:—*
Follow the procedure as in para. 3, but remove the firing pin from the bolt-head after the latter has been unscrewed.

5. *To strip the backsight:—*
Remove the washer pin, washer, axis pin, and leaf.
Press the slide catch screw, and remove the slide from the leaf.
Unscrew the slide catch screw, and remove the spring and catch.
* *Remove the fixing pin, windgauge screw head and spring.*
* *Unscrew the wind-gauge screw and remove the wind-gauge and spring.*
Remove the screw and spring from the bed.
N.B.—The sight bed must not be removed from serviceable rifles.
*Does not apply to No. 1 "B." leaf, which has a fixed cap secured by a screw.

6. *To strip magazines of rifles No. 1:—*
No. 1 "A",—Turn the stop dip down to the front of the magazine. Depress the rear end of the platform and draw the platform forward; the platform and spring may then be withdrawn from the case; force off the auxiliary spring and, only when actually necessary, slightly raise the spring clips on the underside of the platform, and remove the string.

No. 1 "B."—Depress the rear end of the platform as far as possible, at the same time holding up the front end; then pull the

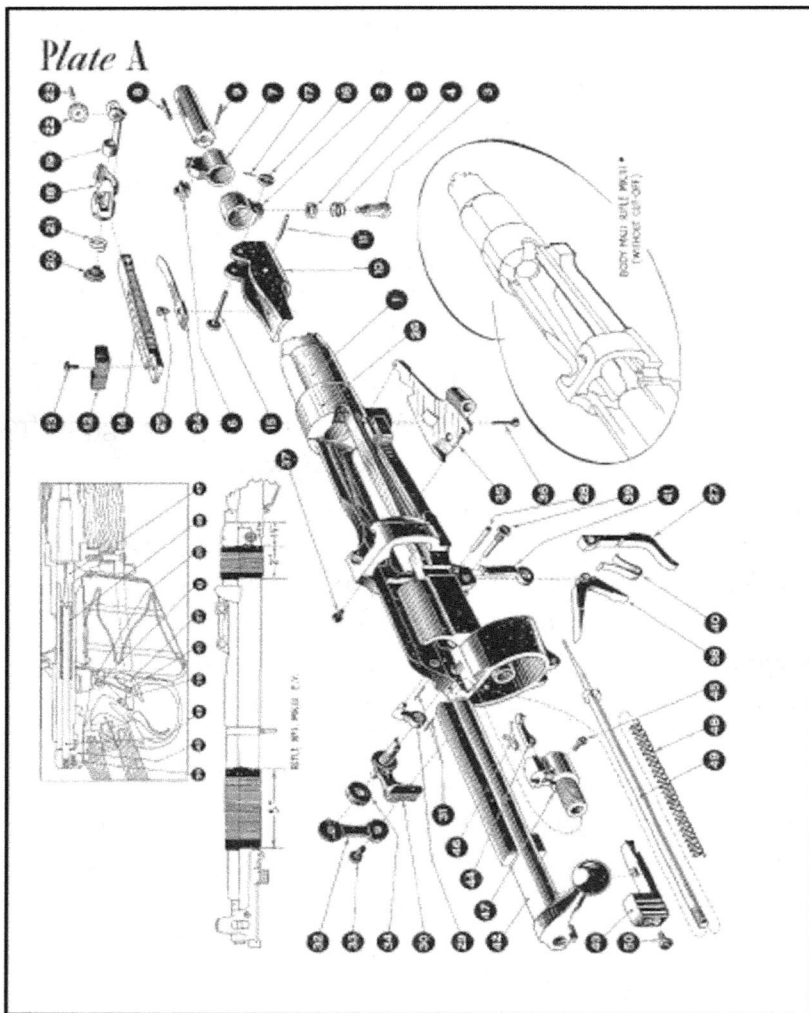

Plate A

front end towards the rear end of, the case, passing it under the front side lips and forcing it between the inner forward ribs of the case. The front end of the platform should then rise up out of the case. Then tilt the rear end of the platform sideways— left side uppermost —and draw it forward out of the case.

4

To Reassemble Rifles
No. 1, Mks. III and III*, and Rifles No. 2, Mk IV*

I. *Magazine of rifles No. 1:*—
Where necessary replace the platform spring in the plat-form, and close down the clips.
Replace the auxiliary spring.
Replace the platform in the magazine, and turn the stop clip (No. 1 "A" magazine only) upwards to retain it.

2. *Backsight:*—
Replace the windgauge, spring and screw.
Replace the spring and screw head, and, after ensuring that the positioning lines on the head and windgauge screw coincide, insert the fixing pin.
Replace the catch, spring and screw in the slide.
Replace the slide on the leaf.
Replace the sight leaf on the bed, and insert the axis pin from the left side.
Replace the washer and washer pin.
Replace the spring and screw in the bed.
•Not for No. 1 'B" leaf.

3. *Locking bolt and safety catch:*—
Place the safety catch on the stem of the locking bolt so that the line marked across the face of the catch is parallel with the flat at the end of the locking bolt. When the safety catch is screwed home, the top end should be in line with the rear end of the thumb piece on the locking bolt.

4. *Bolt of rifles No. 1*
Replace the mainspring and striker in the bolt, then place the cocking-piece in position on the bolt, ensuring that the stud is in

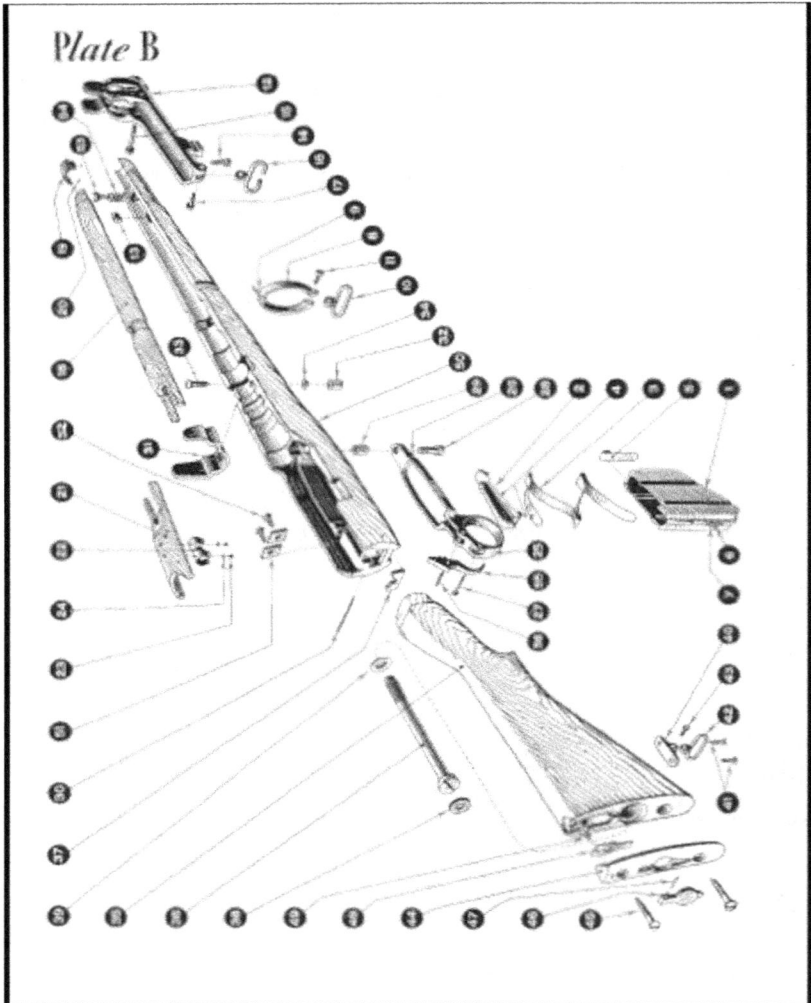

Plate B

the long cam; screw home the striker until the end is flush with the rear end of the cocking-piece and the keeper screw recess is in its correct position; replace the keeper screw, and screw home the bolt head. Turn the cocking-piece into the long cam, and gauge the height of the striker point from the face of the bolt-head.

5. *Bolt of rifles No. 2, Mk. IV*:—*

Proceed as in para. 4, but before assembling the bolt-head, see that the firing pin is inserted, that it is quite free, and that its rear end does not project beyond the end of the bolt-head tenon when the firing pin is in its most forward position. When gauging the height of the firing pin point, the bolt should be held vertically firing pin upward. The projection should be the same as for No. 1 rifles.

6. *The rifles:*—
Replace the sight leaf.
Replace the magazine catch and pin.
Replace the sear, retaining spring, sear screw, and spring.
Replace the cut-off and screw (rifles No. 1, Mk. III only).
Replace the safety catch, locking bolt, washer or aperture sight, spring and screw.

Assemble the stock butt to the body, and screw home the stock bolt, seeing that the square end of the bolt protrudes through the face of the body within the limits of the gauge supplied, and that it is in the correct position for the keeper plate.

Replace the wad, butt plate and butt plate screws.
* *Replace the protector, screw, and nut on the fore-end.*
Replace the fore-end, taking care that the inner band and the fore-end stud and spring are in their correct position in recesses in the fore-end.
Replace the inner band spring and screw.
Replace the trigger, and trigger pin in the guard.
Replace the trigger guard, and screws, back and front.
Replace the magazine.
Replace the hand guard, rear.
Replace the hand guard, front (with cap and screw assembled).
Replace the outer band, swivel and screw.
Replace the nose-cap and screws, front and back.
Replace the extractor, screw and spring.
Replace the bolt in the body—*see* para. 7.

7. *To replace the bolt:*—
See that the resisting lug and cocking-piece are in a straight line, and that the bolt-head is screwed home. Place the bolt in the body with the extractor upward, push forward the bolt till the head is clear of the resisting shoulder,

turn the bolt-head down to the right, press it over the retaining spring, close the breech, and press the trigger.

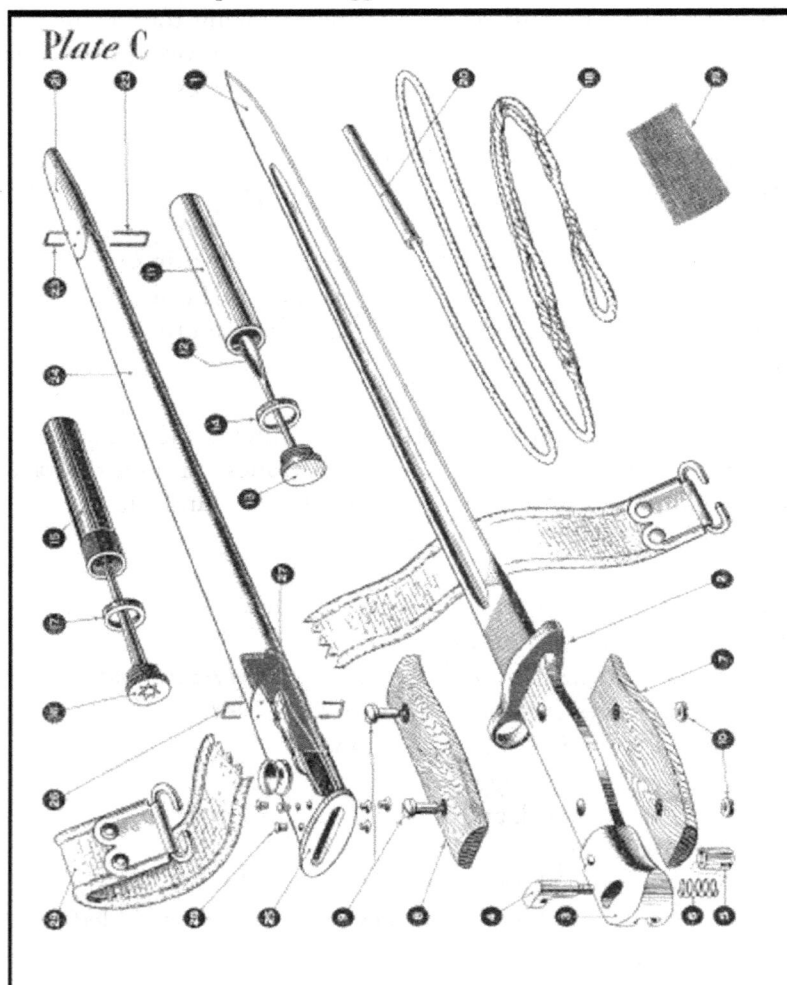

Plate C

To Strip Rifles No. 3

1. *Remove in following order:—*
Bolt.
Nose-cap screw, band screw, and swivel.
Magazine plate, spring, and platform.
* In rifles of early manufacture fitted with long-range sights, replace
the dial sight fixing screw and washer also, if detached.
Screws trigger guard. back and front.
Trigger guard with magazine catch, and magazine case.
Nose-cap from the stock, and handguard, front.
Band and handguard, rear.
Barrel and body from the stock.
Sear axis pin, sear, with spring, and trigger.
Bolt stop screw, bolt stop, with spring and ejector, and aperture sight.
* Safety catch, locking bolt cover plate, locking bolt and spring.
† Backsight axis screw, nut and leaf.
Screw and spring from the backsight bed.

2. *To remove the bolt from the rifle:—*
Withdraw the bolt to its full extent; pull outwards the thumb-piece of
the bolt stop and draw the bolt out of the body.

3. *To strip the bolt:—*
Turn the extractor to the right until it covers the gas escape hole and
the nib is clear of the cannelure, and push the extractor forward.
With a piece of string round the stripping nib, or with the "Tool,
stripping, bolt," if available, draw out the cocking-piece so that the
tooth is clear of the rear end of the bolt, and then unscrew the bolt
plug, Place the point of the striker on a piece of hard wood, press
down the bolt plug until the rear end is clear of the cocking-piece,
give the cocking-piece a quarter turn and lift it off the striker, Let the
bolt plug rise slowly and remove it and the mainspring from the

striker. Care should be taken not to let the bolt plug slip when the mainspring is compressed.

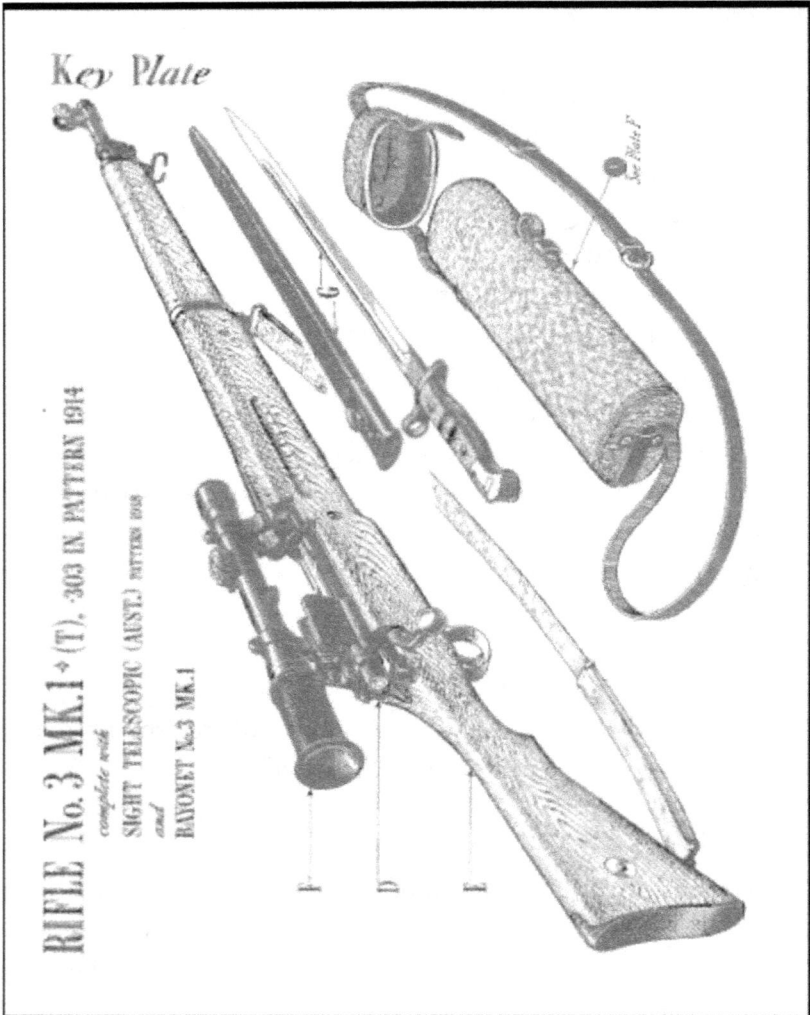

Key Plate

RIFLE No.3 MK.1*(T). .303 IN. PATTERN 1914
complete with
SIGHT TELESCOPIC (AUST.) PATTERN 1918
and
BAYONET No.3 MK.1

See Plate F

4. *To remove the block, band, foresight, from the barrel:—*
Drive out the fixing pin from right to left.
Remove the block by gently tapping it with a mallet towards the muzzle end of the barrel.

Take the key from the seating.

Note. — The block is never to be removed from the barrel except when it becomes necessary to exchange the nose-cap, or handguard ring.

5. *To remove the safety catch:*—
Turn the safety catch backward until the thumb-piece is in the lowest position and pull it outward, slightly oscillating the thumb-piece during withdrawal.

* The safety catch must be removed before removing the locking bolt cover plate in order to prevent the locking bolt from flying out of its housing. In "W" rifles of early manufacture, the cover plate is dovetailed into the body from the underside.

* The end of the axis screw is riveted over the nut; when removing the nut, care must be taken to avoid breaking off the end of the screw.

5. *To remove the magazine plate, spring and platform:*—
With the point of a bullet, depress the magazine catch and slide the bottom plate backward; the three parts will then come out together. Slide the ends of the spring out of the recesses in the plate and platform, raising the bent ends to allow the spring to move backwards.

To Re-assemble Rifles No. 3

1. *To re-assemble the magazine platform and spring to the plate:*—
Slide the narrow end of the spring into the recess on the platform. Slide the wide end of the spring into the recess on the bottom plate.

2. *To replace the magazine plate:*—
Insert the platform and spring into the magazine case, press the plate flat on the trigger guard and slide it forward, noting that the catch rises to engage and lock the plate in position.

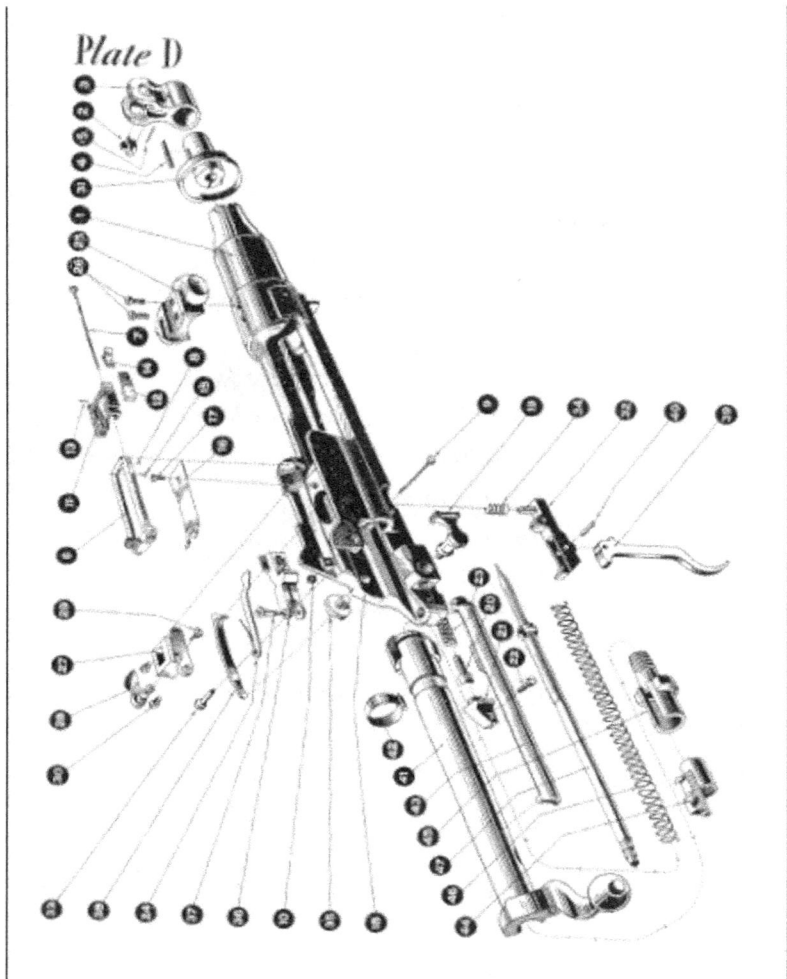

Plate D

3. *To re-assemble the locking bolt and safety catch:*—

Replace the locking bolt (with V-groove horizontal) and spring in the housing, and push forward as far as possible with a thin drift inserted through the hole at the rear of the housing. Hold the safety catch in a position which allows the flat of the half moon to lie horizontally, with the thumb-piece pointing downward (the half moon must pass over the drift); push the safety catch home and withdraw the drift smartly.

4. *To re-assemble the bolt:*—Place the point of the striker on a piece of hard wood, replace the mainspring and slightly compress it. Place the bolt plug in position with the flattened sides of the hole in line with the flats on the striker. Force the bolt plug down as far as possible and grip it firmly. Place the cocking-piece in position with the flats inside the cylindrical portion in line with the flats on striker, push the cocking-piece down until its rear end is flush with the rear end of the striker. Give the cocking-piece a quarter turn, so that the tooth is in line with the slot in the bolt plug, which can then be allowed to rise.

Place the striker and mainspring inside the bolt and screw the bolt plug into the, bolt, drawing back the cocking-piece clear of the rear end of the bolt with a piece of string or with the "Tool, stripping, bolt," if available, until the tooth is directly behind the short groove.

Slide on the extractor so that the undercut portion passes over the lugs on the ring. Lift the retaining nib over the face of the bolt and into the cannelure (care being taken not to overstrain and set the extractor), and turn the extractor so that it lies over the solid lug on the right of the bolt.

5. *To replace the block, band, foresight on the barrel:*—
Replace the key in the seating, seeing that the pin groove coincides with the pin groove in the barrel. Replace the block, and, if necessary, gently tap it with a mallet until the fixing pin hole coincides with the pin grooves in the barrel and key. Insert the fixing pin from left to right, and gently tap it home into position.

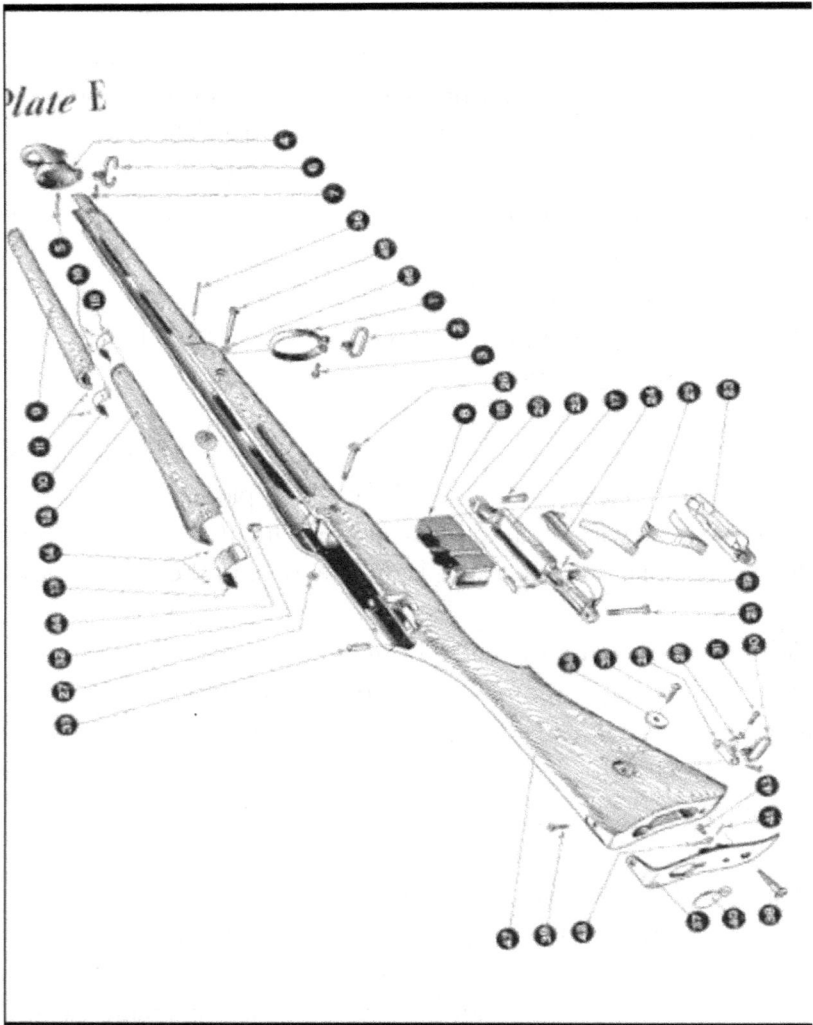

During the operation of removing and replacing, care must be taken not to damage the key and pin. Blocks are not interchangeable and are fitted to barrels on first assembly. It is therefore essential, when a block is removed from a barrel, that it should be re-assembled to the same barrel; in order to ensure this, the block should be immediately replaced on the barrel, from which it was removed even though the replacement of the nose-cap and handguard ring has to be carried out later.

6. *To assemble the rifle:*—
Replace in the following order:—
Spring and screw in the backsight bed.
Leaf, axis screw, and nut.
Locking bolt and spring; safety catch and locking bolt cover plate.
Aperture sight, bolt stop spring*, ejector, bolt stop, and screw.
Trigger, sear spring, sear, and sear axis pin.
Barrel and body in the stock, lubricating with mineral jelly as required.
Rear handguard, lower band, front handguard, and nose-cap.
* Magazine case, trigger guard and screws front and back.
Magazine plate, spring, and platform.

Lower band screw and swivel and nose-cap screw.
It is essential that the outer face at the front end of the bolt stop ring should be flush with the outer face of the bolt stop, and not below latter, otherwise the front end bearing of the spring may be sheared during movement of the bolt stop, and the rifle rendered unusable.
*Care should be taken when assembling that the projection at the top front end of the magazine-case is correctly positioned in the recess under the body before the trigger guard is screwed up.

7. *To replace the bolt in the rifle:*—
See that the bolt plug is screwed home, that the tooth on the front end of the cocking-piece is engaged in the short groove on the end of the bolt, and that the extractor is in direct line with the solid lug on the right of the bolt Insert the bolt in the body of the rifle, depress the platform and press the bolt home.

SECTION 2.
Cleaning and Lubricating of Rifles in use,
and the Clearing of Obstructions from the Bore

Note.—The lubricating oil referred to in this section, and elsewhere as "G.S.," is termed M/80 in the V.A.O.S.

1. The rifles are to be kept in a clean condition, special attention being given to the interior of the barrel and the breech action. Instructions for the care and cleaning of rifles by troops are contained in Small Arms Training, Vol. I, 1924, Chapter II Sections 38-40. Armourers should make themselves thoroughly acquainted with these instructions in addition to the instructions given hereunder.

2. Oil, lubricating, G.S., only is to be used for cleaning the action; the use of abrasive substances, such as emery and emery cloth, is forbidden.

3. To prevent water soaking into the stock, and at the same time to give the latter a polished appearance, it should be well rubbed with oil. French polish or varnish is on no account to be used. Red mineral jelly should be applied between stock, handguards, barrel and body as a protection against rust. At stations abroad, a mixture of two parts mineral jelly to one of beeswax will be employed.

4. *To clean the bore of .303-inch barrels:—*
5. Oil, lubricating, G.S., only is to be used, but mineral burning oil (paraffin) can be mixed with it, as necessary, when cleaning with brass wire and with jute and emery, as detailed below.

6. To clean a slightly rusty barrel with the double pull through, remove the bolt and nose-cap, drop the pull- through weight through the barrel from the breech, clamp the muzzle guide on the muzzle of the barrel to prevent damage by the friction of the cord, well oil the gauze wire, and, with the necessary assistance, pull the gauze wire to and fro until the rust is removed. Care must be taken to draw the

pull- through out of the barrel in line with the bore, as friction between the pull through cord and the wall of the chamber at the breech will cause the chamber to become oval and thus render the barrel unserviceable. When, in consequence of frequent use, the gauze wire ceases to fit the barrel tightly, narrow strips of the gauze, about -inch wide, or flannelette or paper, may be inserted under each side to increase its diameter.

7. To clean rusty barrels with brass wire, emery and jute, fill the eye of the No. 4 rod with from 50 to 60 strands of the hard brass wire, No. 26 W.G., supplied in 3-inch lengths, and press the ends-well back along the rod. The rifles must then be held in a vice, and, after the nose cap has been removed, the wire, well oiled with a mixture of two parts of "Oil, lubricating, G.S.," to one part of paraffin oil, is inserted in the muzzle end of the barrel; the muzzle guide * is then clamped on the muzzle and the rod worked up and down the bore to remove the rust. When a barrel is very rusty, it will found easier to loosen the rust by plugging the muzzle of the barrel, pouring in paraffin oil from the breech end, and leaving it there for a few hours. After loosening the rust, wipe out the barrel with jute inserted in the No. 1 rod and examine (the jute should be cut in lengths of about 8 inches). If a barrel is found to require further cleaning, coil the jute round so that it fits the bore tightly, sprinkle on a little flour emery, replace it in the barrel, and after clamping on the muzzle guide, work the rod well up and down until the barrel is clean. A slightly pitted surface will usually remain; this should be oiled with "Oil, lubricating, G.S." To preserve the wire on the No. 4 rod when not in use, a cartridge case cut short at the shoulder will be found useful as a cap. The length of the No.4 rod is such as will ensure that the wire will not pass beyond the front end of the chamber and become jammed. The No. 1 rod, for jute, is of a suitable length to pass through the barrel from the breech end.

8. When rifles are received from store, and the bore of the barrel is

thickly coated with mineral jelly, the latter must be removed and the bore lightly oiled with G.S. oil before the rifles are issued to troops. When a muzzle guide becomes badly worn in the cleaning rod guide bole, and no longer protects the bore of the barrel, it should be exchanged.

9. *To clean the chamber of .303-inch barrels:*—
Use only a piece of gauze wire, or a piece of oiled flannelette, necessary, in the chamber cleaning stick. Care must be taken not to enlarge or damage the chamber by the use of unauthorized materials. A bright chamber is not to be insisted upon.

10. *To clean the bore of rifles No. 2, Mk. IV (.22-inch):*—
The No. 6 rod with leather washer, and the brass cleaner for flannelette, and the brush, which are made to screw on to the rod, are provided for the use of units in possession of these rifles. Oil, lubricating, G.S., only is to be used for cleaning purposes. When proper care is taken by units to clean and oil the bore immediately after firing, the barrels can be kept in good condition. Armourers should draw the attention of the responsible officer concerned to the fact when the barrels are not kept in good order. In the event of an obstruction, such as flannelette, etc., being found in the bore, great care must be taken not to put excessive pressure on the rod, as damage to the bore may thereby be caused. If the obstruction cannot readily be removed by the armourer, a report will be rendered in order that the matter may be investigated and the rifle sent to C.I.S.A. for special examination.

11. *To clear .303-inch barrels when a pull through has broken and become jammed in the bore:*—
Screw the "tool plug" on the "rod," place it in the barrel at the end nearest the jammed flannelette and compress the flannelette and cord as much as possible. Withdraw the rod and plug, unscrew the plug, and screw on the bush and screw bit. Pass this into the barrel at the

end nearest the jammed flannelette and turn it to the right, pressing it firmly against the jammed material until a good hold is obtained, then pull strongly on the rod, causing the screw to grip tightly in the material by turning the rod whilst pulling.

Note.—Only the hardened steel rods issued are to be used for cleaning and clearing purposes; Rods of soft metal or wood must on no account be employed.

SECTION 3.—EXAMINATION
Rifles No. 1 and No. 2, Mk. IV*

The following instructions are for general guidance; the sequence may be varied to meet special circumstances, *e.g.*, when a particular defect due to unfair wears or other cause is prevalent, or when a brief examination only is called for. Reference should be made to Section 4 for Modifications,
Repairs and Adjustments and to Chapter III, Part I, for special markings.

1. General.—Examine the rifle to see that the number, and the series letter where marked, on the nose-cap, fore-end, sight leaf, barrel and bolt agree with the number on the body, and that the rifle is complete. Record deficiencies, if any and damage due to unfair wear for report.

2. *Barrels.*—(i) Examine the bore and chamber. Rust, bulges, bad cuts, cord-wear and bends should be looked for, and should be reported in the normal manner. Slight rust pitting in the chamber may be ignored except in cases where hard extraction has been reported. The gauges for bore and lead are available under the conditions laid down in E.R., Pt. I, and there is any doubt by the unit as to the accuracy of shooting, the barrel should gauged as follows:—

.303-inch plug should run.
.307-inch plug should not run.
.308-inch plug should not enter the muzzle more than ¼ inch.
.310-inch plug should not enter the breech more than ¼ inch (i.e., the rear end of the gauge should not pass inside the barrel.)

Note.—(a) Each limit gauge for the bore, also the lead gauge, independently determines the normal life of the barrel, but, should the rifle still be shooting accurately, the armourer will use his discretion before reporting the barrel as unserviceable.

(*b*) When a rifle shoots inaccurately, and the barrel is the gauging limits, and the stocking correct, it will be reported for special examination by C.I.S.A.

Test the backsight bed and foresight band block for rigidity, and the foresight blade for security. Slight lateral movement in the bed and block, provided it is insufficient to affect sighting and accuracy, may be ignored. Blades, foresight, known as Mk. II, introduced in India, having a base of .03 inch wider than that of Mk. I foresights to enable them to be set to a maximum of .045 inch off centre, may be met with in rifles brought home in the past by troops. Such foresights may remain until exchange for another height is necessary when they will be replaced by the ordinary service No. 1 pattern. The Mk.II sights are stamped with the figure 2 alongside the H, N or L marking.

Barrels of rifles No. 2 (.22-inch)—Will be examined without gauges. Special attention will be paid to the muzzle in order that wear resulting from careless use of the cleaning rod may be detected, and to the chamber at the end of the extractor way, where burrs are liable to be caused by the extractor. A burr at this point may affect extraction, and should be removed by means of a keen-edged scraper. Care must be taken to avoid enlargement of or damage to the chamber. When a .22-inch barrel is found on examination to be eroded or worn to such an extent that accuracy may be affected, its condition will be reported to the responsible officer concerned in order that the rifle may be tested for accuracy. When a rifle fails to group within the prescribed limits, it will be reported for special examination by C.I.S.A. (*see* Small Arms Training). If it appears that proper care is not being taken in the cleaning and oiling of these rifles, a report will be rendered to the responsible officer concerned to this effect, and a copy of the report will be retained for future reference.

3. *Butt, fore-end and handguards.*—Examine for damage, splits, warping, excessive dryness or rot, and, especially at sea coast stations, for salt deposit; evidence of the latter will usually be indicated by rust on the barrel. Where salt deposit is distinctly in evidence, the fore-end and .handguards should be replaced. See that the butt is firmly held in the body, and that the correct stocking conditions are maintained; where the parts are patched, see that the patches are secure.

Note.—A split at the rear end of the fore-end, at the junction portion under the stock bolt plate may be ignored, provided the screwed wire has a firm hold. If the stocking is satisfactory, lubricate, as required, with red mineral jelly, or, at stations abroad, with a mixture of two parts mineral jelly to one part beeswax.

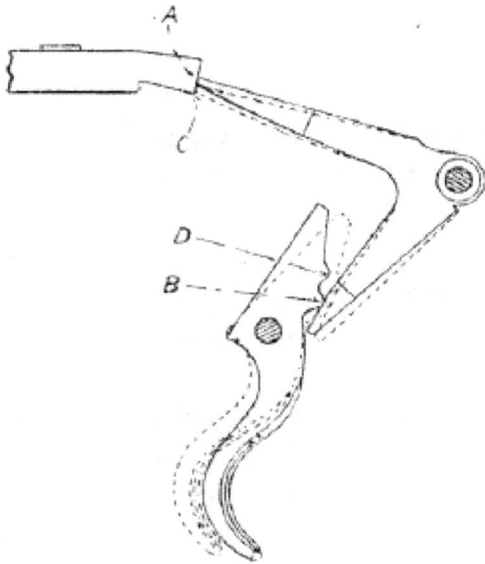

Fig. 1.

4. *Action:*—*Bolt and bolt-head.*

(1)Test the distance of the bolt from the end of the chamber with gauges .064-inch No. 1 and .074-inch No. 1; the bolt should close

23

over the .064, but not over the .074; when using the latter gauge, light thumb-pressure only should be applied to the knob. Also test to see that the wing of the bolt-head does not lift off the rib of the body.

(ıı)Examine the bolt for fracture and damage, especially at the cocking cam and recoil shoulders. Test the striker for free movement and fit in the cocking-piece: gauge the length and radius of the striker point; examine the bents and condition of the cam stud of the cocking-piece.

(ııı)Test the fit of the bolt-head in the bolt, and examine the face for erosion; when erosion is excessive or the rib turns beyond the rib of the bolt freely, fit a longer bolt-head and adjust to the 064 gauge as necessary.

(ıϖ)Examine the extractor at the hook and for fit on the screw, and test to see that the screw is secure. Weigh the spring from the hook with the trigger tester - not less than 6 lb. and not more than 9 lb. should be required to move it.

Note.—The bolts of rifles in use should be completely stripped at each annual examination and lubricated lightly with G.S. oil.

Body, etc.—Examine the body of No. 1 rifles for fracture, especially in the region of the recoil shoulders; test the charger guide bridge for security if oil exudes at the rivets, but no appreciable looseness is found, no action is necessary; test to see that the retaining spring is held rigidly by the sear screw. Examine the sear and magazine catch for condition and free movement, and oil, as required.

Gauge the protrusion of the stock bolt and see that the squared end is correctly located for the keeper plate in the fore-end.

Locking bolt and safety catch.—Examine for fracture and wear, and test for functioning in both cocked and fired positions of the rifle; see that the locking bolt spring is held firmly by the screw and that the screw is secured.

Pull-off, spring weights, etc., will be tested with the trigger tester as follows:—

Limits Minimum Maximum
To release the bolt-head from the retaining spring 10 lb. 16 lb.
To draw back the cocking-piece against the mainspring—
(*a*) in the fired position 7 lb. 9 lb.
(*b*) at full cock 14 lb. 16 lb.

Pull-off—
(*a*) first pull 3 lb. 4 lb.
(*b*) second pull 5 lb. 6 lb.
To lift the butt trap at the nib 2 lb. 3 lb.

Both first and second pulls should be tested by hand to ensure that they are correct and smooth in operation. The safety of the engagement of the sear nose with the bent of the cocking-piece should be tested by forcing the bolt home as sharply as possible.

The engagement of the half-bent of the cocking-piece with the nose of the sear should be tested by only partially closing the bolt, so that on pulling the trigger, the stud of the cocking- piece will rest on the end of the cam stud of the bolt. Upon releasing the trigger and fully closing the bolt, the sear should securely engage in the half bent; it should not then be possible to disengage the sear by pressure on the trigger.

Cut-off of No. 1, Mk. III rifles.—Examine for damage, and test the action when the magazine is empty and when filled with dummy cartridges. Where the cut-off is of an earlier pattern than No. 1 i.e., with the short stops at the rear end) and the end of the slot in the body is so worn as to render the stops ineffective, the cut-off should be exchanged for a No. 1.

Magazine of No. 1 rifles.—Examine for damage; see that the platform spring is securely held in the platform, and that the auxiliary spring is secure. See that the case is securely held by the magazine catch, and then test the feed into the chamber when filled as above.

Note.—The magazine-case only, marked .22 on the left side, is used in No. 2, Mk. IV* rifles.

Extraction end ejection.—These functions can be observed when testing the magazine; tests should be carried out also with fired cartridge-cases. The action of the lug of the bolt on the extracting cam of the body should withdraw the bolt from .08 to .10 inch. A rifle having this amount of draw should not fail to extract provided the action is otherwise correct. In case of failure to extract a tight cartridge-case under the normal conditions of operation, the following points should be looked for:—

(i) play between bolt and bolt-head;
(ii) play at extractor axis;
(ııı)excessive clearance between extractor hook and rim of cartridge.

Replacement of the part or parts found to be noticeably worn should be made as necessary to effect a remedy. When ejection is unsatisfactory, examine the ejector screw and the lower corner of the extractor, and test the weight of the extractor spring; if the corner of the extractor is sharp, it should be slightly rounded off.

Note.—The foregoing applies more especially to No. 1 rifles. In the case of No. 2 rifles, the condition of the ex- tractor hook and its engagement with the rim of fired cases should receive attention. See also that the extractor does not foul the edge of the extractor way of the barrel.

5. *Freedom of the muzzle of the barrel and fit of the bayonet.* — Insert a hard wood plug in the muzzle of the barrel and test to see that the barrel is free in the nose-cap and that it is pressed upward by the stud and spring. If the bayonet is very slack on the nose-cap, exchange the bayonet for a closer- fitting one off another rifle on which the slack bayonet is a better fit, and then re-number the bayonets to the rifles.

6. *Securing screws.*—Before re-issue of rifles to troops, see that they are complete, and then expand the swivel screws and secure the front trigger-guard screw.

Note— If complaint is made of misfires occurring in any No. 1 rifle, the point of impact of the striker on the fired cases should be examined; when found badly eccentric, the rifle should be set aside for special gauging by the A.I.A. or C.I.S.A.'s Examiners at their next visit. Should, however, the rifle be urgently required, it can be sent to C.I.S.A. for special examination. In the absence of fired cases, a dummy cartridge, with cap chamber filled with beeswax, will serve the purpose.

Rifles No. 3, Mk. I* (T) and Mk. I* (F)

These rifles will be examined on similar lines to those for Nos. 1 and 2 rifles, but special care must be taken with them, especially with Mk. I* (T) rifles fitted with telescopic sight, in view of the importance of the accuracy of shooting required for "sniping" and of the high standard of adjustment attained before the rifles are issued from the ordnance factory.

The instructions given in Sections 1, 2 and 4 contain the information necessary for general guidance when examining these rifles. *See also*

Section 6- Gauges .064. No. 2 and .074-inch No, 2 and application of plug and rod gauges to barrel.

SECTION 4.

Repairs, Modifications and Adjustments
Rifles No. 1, Mk. III and III* and No. 2 Mk. IV*

1. *Misfires.*—When misfires have been reported with any rifle, the mainspring should be weighed and the protrusion of the striker gauged. It is also possible for the force of the striker blow to be reduced by an accumulation of oil in the spring chamber of the bolt. If the impression made by the striker on the cap is notice-ably out of centre, the rifle should be placed on one side for special examination, as directed in Section 3.

2. *Fitting new ejector screw.*—When fitting a new ejector screw, see that the end of the screw just touches the bolt in its passage, but not sufficiently to cause appreciable friction.

3. *Fitting new striker.*—When fitting a new striker, care must be taken to adjust it for length to the gauge striker point; the point should be carefully rounded to the radius in the gauge, a long or badly rounded striker is liable to cause pierced caps.

4. *To tighten striker in cocking-piece.*—Take an unserviceable cocking-piece with the thread for the striker in good condition; split it with the slitting saw down the centre, tap with the plug tap No. 10, and harden and temper. Then screw in the loose striker until the rear end protrudes a little beyond the rear end of the cocking-piece, grip the cocking piece in the vice, and centre-punch the centre of the end of the striker, or otherwise expand the metal; then unscrew the striker and remove any burr or superfluous metal from the end.

5. *Fitting new platform and spring to No. 1 "A" magazine of rifles No. 1.* — (Platforms and springs for No. 1 "B" magazines are not issued

separately.) Insert the spring under the nibs of the platform with the raised stop on the spring between the nibs, and close the nibs down tightly on the spring, seeing that the spring is in line with the platform and held tightly. In rifles of all patterns, work the spring and platform in the magazine until they raise the cartridges freely.

6. *To increase or decrease the weight of the pull-off and to produce and regulate the double pull.* -

To reduce the weight, increase, with an oilstone, the angle made with the vertical by the face of the bent "A" (Fig. 1). To increase the weight reduce the angle. When fitting a new sear, trigger, or trigger guard, the double pull will be regulated, as necessary, in the following manner.

Remove the fore-end from the rifle, insert the new sear in the body, the new trigger in the guard or the old trigger in the new guard, withdraw the front guard screw collar from the fore-end, assemble the guard with the collar in position under the guard and fully cock the bent "A" (Fig. 1) shows the correct position of the sear nose on the end of the cocking- piece at full cock. Upon pulling the trigger, the rib on the trigger at "B" coming in contact with the sear, draws the sear down to the position shown at "C"; the rib on the trigger at "D" then comes in contact with the sear and draws the sear off the cocking-piece. If the sear is drawn off the cocking-piece by the first action of the trigger, and there is no second pull, the height of the rib "B." should be reduced with oilstone or emery cloth until the sear assumes the correct position, as shown at "C," care being taken to maintain the shape.

Note.—Before removing the front guard screw collar from the fore-end, see that the ends of the collar are flush with the fore-end; if the collar is short, replace it, as otherwise a false result will be obtained for the Pull-off.

7. *To fit new bolt-head to Rifles No.* 1.—(Spare part bolt- heads, marked "S" on the top, are longer at the front.) Assemble the bolt-head to the bolt, insert it in the body, and test with .064-inch No. 1 gauge; should the bolt not close over the gauge, remove the bolt-head from the bolt, and having placed a piece of emery cloth (No. F) on a flat surface, rub the face of the bolt-head on the emery cloth, maintaining a circular motion in order to preserve a flat surface, until sufficient metal has been removed to enable the assembled bolt to close over the gauge.

8.The bolt should not close over the .074-inch No. 1 gauge. Care should be taken to keep the-face of the bolt-head flat and square. After fitting and adjusting, the top front edge of the face of the bolt-head is to be rounded to a radius not exceeding .02-inch.

Note.—When it is found that the bolts of several rifles turn over the 074-inch No. 1 gauge, the bolt-heads should be exchanged among such rifles, as, owing to the varying lengths of bodies and bolts, bolt-heads which are too short in one rifle may be serviceable in another. Bolt-heads that have been replaced in rifles by longer ones, should be kept by the armourer and used whenever possible in rifles requiring the bolt-head replaced, so as to avoid unnecessary use of new spare part bolt-heads. Part-worn bolt-heads held as required by armourers in accordance with the foregoing need not be accounted for as part of the annual allowance of new spare parts.

8. *Instructions for fitting new No.* 2 *bolt-heads and firing-pins to rifles No.* 2, *Mk. IV*.*—(a) Assemble the bolt-head to the rifle without the firing-pin, and adjust the front face, where necessary, to enable the bolt to be closed with the bolt-head touching the face of the barrel.

(*b*) Remove the bolt-head from the rifle, insert the firing-pin, and press home to the small shoulder (A) (Fig. 2). If the rear end (B) of the pin is found to project beyond the rear face (C) of the bolt-head, reduce the pin at (B) until it is just below the face (C). This ensures that the bolt-head, and not the small shoulder (D) of the firing-pin, acts as a stop to the forward movement of the striker.

(c) Assemble the bolt complete; place the cocking-piece in the long cam of the bolt; test the protrusion of the point of the firing-pin, which should be the same as in the Service rifle (i.e.,.04 inch to .042 inch),and adjust the point where necessary, maintaining the radial form at the point, as illustrated.

Note.—The internal shoulder (A) in the bolt-head controls the firing-pin in its most forward position, and when the firing- pin is properly adjusted1 prevents it from striking the edge of the chamber when snapping. Therefore, when adjusting the rear-end (B) of the firing-pin, care should be taken to see that the pin is not more than .003 inch below the rear face (C) of the bolt-head, as whatever distance it is below, so there will exist a similar clearance between the shoulder (D) of the pin and the shoulder (A) of the bolt-head when the pin is gauged for protrusion, and this, added to the amount of protrusion as gauged, gives the amount of protrusion of the striker point in its most forward position.

To re-line the windgauge or cap of the back sight of rifles No. 1 and No. 2.

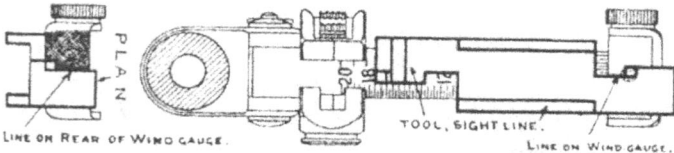

LINE ON REAR OF WIND GAUGE.　　TOOL, SIGHT LINE.　　LINE ON WIND GAUGE.

Fig. 3.

Tool, sight line, and scriber will be used in the following manner and as shown in Fig. 3.

First re-brown the windgauge, assemble it to the No.1 "A" sight leaf, and adjust it to its central position, i.e., with the original top centre line (now browned over, but visible) in correct alignment with the centre line on the leaf, and with the windgauge screw spring engaged in a notch in the screw-head. Next place the sight line tool over the wind- gauge and leaf, and see if the lines on the windgauge are in correct alignment with the tool; reverse the tool to verify. Then, with the scriber (which should not be too sharp), trace over to brighten the lines at the front and top of the wind- gauge, reversing the tool as necessary.

The above instructions, so far as they apply, will be followed when re-lining the fixed cap of the No. 1 "B" leaf.

10. *Fitting washers to take up backlash of the windgauge screw fitted to No. 1 "A" "sight leaf.*—In cases where back- lash of the windgauge screw exists, owing to the distance between the removable head of the windgauge screw and the right side of the windgauge being too great, one or more washers, .005-inch thick, will be placed in the recess on the left side of the windgauge under the small slotted head of the windgauge screw. Before fitting the washers, care should be taken to see that the backlash is not due to any defect of the windgauge Screw spring, which, if defective, should be exchanged.

11. *Fitting a No.1 head to the windgauge screw of No.1 "A" sight leaf*-When fitting the No. 1 head to the windgauge screw of rifles fitted with slides of earlier manufacture, a radial groove is to be filed in the right rear side of the slide, at "A," Fig, 4, to give clearance to the No. 1 head, which is larger than the earlier pattern. The depth to which the groove is to be filed will be determined by trying the slide on the sight leaf (assembled with windgauge and screw with No.1 head) until it can be set just below the 200 yards position.

NOT LESS THAN ·02 THICK.

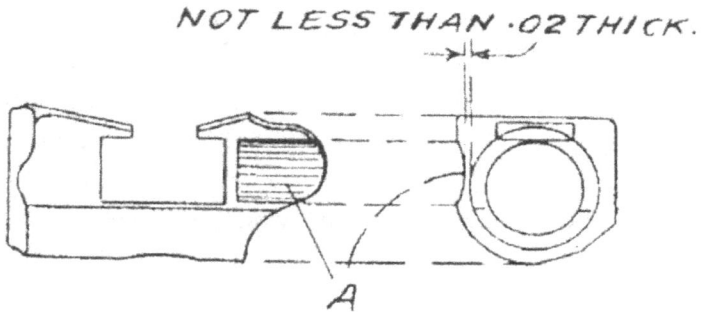

Fig. 4.

Alter adjusting the slide to suit the No. 1 head; it will be blacked in accordance with the instructions given for the temporary blacking of sights.

12. *Butts.*—When, owing to shrinkage, the socket end of the butt does not fit the body, the looseness will be remedied by attaching a piece of hard paper to the socket end of the butt. The adhesion and protection of the paper will be effected by applying "hard, white spirit varnish," with a 1-inch camel-hair brush in the following manner:—

Varnish the wood and paper and allow both to be exposed to the air for about 30 seconds, then apply one to the other. When dry, varnish the outside and allow to dry and harden. When fitting the butt to the body, lubricate with red mineral jelly.

In the event of difficulty in attaching the paper, owing to the presence of oil, the socket end of the butt will be cleaned with "oxalic acid," and water (1 ounce acid to 1 pint water). The acid must be washed off with clean water, and the wood thoroughly dried before applying varnish and paper. Since the socket end of the butt is

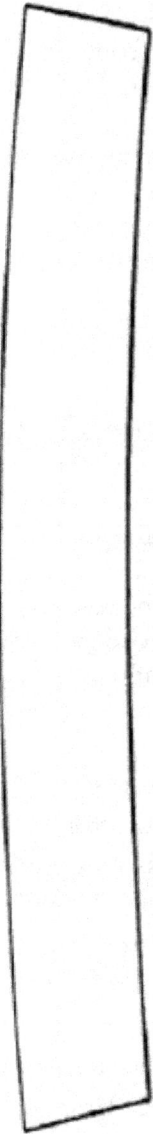

Fig. 5.

tapered, the cutting of the paper will be facilitated by the use of a template made in accordance with Fig. 5. The varnish, brushes and acid will be specially demanded as required. Anvils are provided to drive the butts home into the socket of the body. These anvils will also be used with new butts of which the socket end has been compressed in manufacture and left large for a driving fit.

To fit a new fore-end to rifles No. 1:—
Remove from the unserviceable fore-end:—
(i) The dial sight complete with fixing screw and washer (when fitted to No. 1 "A" fore-ends).
The nose cap nut.
The stock bolt plate.
The collar.
The inner band spring washer.
The protector with screw, nut and washer.
(ii) Select the new fore-end to match reasonably with the butt, and examine it for straightness; assemble the nose-cap with nut and screws, the guard screw collar and stock bolt plate, and examine the location of the barrel hole in the nose cap in relation to the barrel groove in the fore-end.

(iii) Place the front handguard on the fore-end, apply its cap to the recess in the nose-cap, and, if necessary, plane or file the upper surfaces of the fore-end until the cap fits and the handguard lies evenly on the fore-end.

(iv) Remove the nose-cap and coat the seating surfaces of barrel and body with lamp black mixed with G.S. oil. Test the seating of the fore-end, and adjust as necessary, taking care to keep the bottom of the groove level with the bottom of the barrel hole in the nose-cap, using a straightedge of sufficient length for the purpose. The fore-end should seat on the base of the body, especially at the front end for 1 ½ inches at least, on the barrel at the reinforce, and from half an inch in rear of the inner band recess to the nose-cap. The guard screw-collar should bear on the boss of the body; and its outer end should be slightly below the guard seating (about .01 inch). The fore-end must be clear of the barrel from the front of the reinforce up to a point half an inch from the inner band recess; it should fit closely between the sear lugs and the face of the butt socket of the body. The inner band recess should be of sufficient depth to ensure that the inner band can be drawn down on to the barrel.

(v) When the seatings and clearances are satisfactory, press the fore-end on the barrel and body, assemble the trigger- guard and screws, and test to see that the barrel is free and that it seats along the bottom of the groove without undue tension. Test the pull-off for double action and, if unsatisfactory, adjust as necessary— *see* paragraph 6. Assemble the nose-cap and screws, test the alignment of the barrel in the fore-end and the barrel hole in the nose-cap, and, if necessary, adjust the sides of the groove to avoid influence on the straightness of the barrel.

(vi) When satisfactory, remove the fore-end, and assemble the remaining components, seeing that the backsight protector is quite clear of the barrel. Lubricate the barrel and body recesses of the fore-end, the groove of the handguards and the barrel and body, with red mineral jelly (at stations abroad, with the mixture referred to in Section 2). Finally, assemble the fore-end to the rifle, seeing that the inner band spring is free to act, that the barrel can be sprung down fully at the muzzle against the tension of the stud and spring, and that the rear handguard does not prevent the backsight slide from seating on the bed at the lower elevations.

(vii) As accuracy of shooting and sighting may be affected by the new fore-end, the rifle should be submitted to the O.C., the Company or Squadron, etc., for accuracy test, the foresight to be adjusted as necessary. (*See* para. 15.)

(viii) Alterations to be made to No. 1 "B" fore-ends when fitting them to rifles with cut-off (*a*) or aperture sight (*b*) :—

(*a*) The upward extension, on the right side of the stock, which covers the position of the cut-off slot in the body: will be cut away, and an angular recess will be cut to half the depth of the cut-off lug recess, to clear the cut-off joint when the cut-off is opened.

(*b*) The aperture sight will be replaced by the washer, spring, bolt locking, but should this component not be available, the pillar of the aperture sight will be filed off at the base and the base disc used as a washer under the spring.

Securing screws. Upon re-assembling the following screws they should be secured as described.

Screw, guard, trigger, front and screw, spring, bolt locking.—The metal of the components into which the screws assemble will be expanded into the screw driver slots, after the screws have been carefully tightened, by centre-punching, as illustrated (Fig. 6) Care should be exercised when centre-punching to avoid cutting away the metal of the components.

SCREW, GUARD, FRONT.

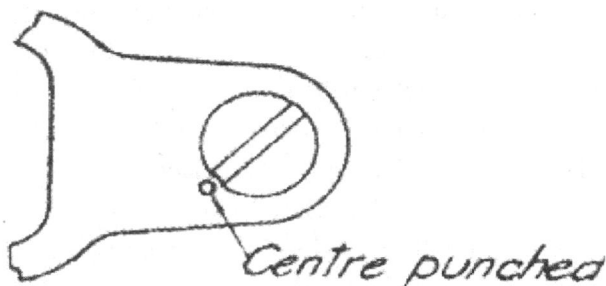

Centre punched

Fig. 6.

Screw, sear.—See that the sear screw is screwed tightly home; make a scriber or pencil mark for the position of the notch on the end of the screw at the bottom edge. Remove the sear screw, and, with a small 3-square file cut a small "V" notch in the end of the screw where marked; replace the screw and screw home tightly; then with the centre-punch, indent the metal of the body into the notch (*see* Fig. 7) and re-assemble the rifle.

Note.—This applies to rifles in use in which the bolt-head retaining spring is not held rigidly owing to the sear screw having worked loose; but it will be carried out also in all rifles undergoing repair and rifles manufactured in future.

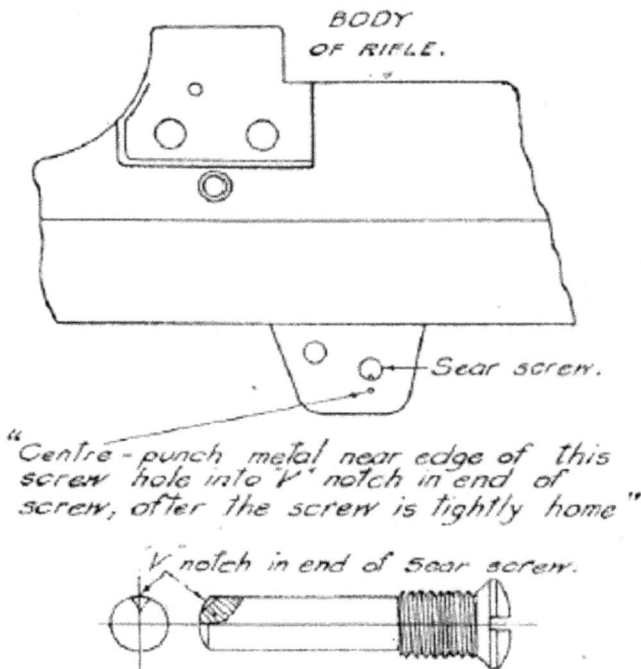

BODY
OF RIFLE.

Sear screw.

"Centre-punch metal near edge of this screw hole into 'V' notch in end of screw, after the screw is tightly home"

V notch in end of Sear screw.

Fig. 7.

Swivel screws.—With the screw head supported conveniently expand the hollow point of the screws, by means of the centre-punch, sufficiently to prevent them from working loose. The expansion must not be overdone, as this will cause damage to the slot when stripping.

15. *To replace and adjust blades foresight.*—Remove the nose cap screws and nose cap. Carefully mark the front end of the blade to be replaced, in line with one edge of the block; drive out the old blade from left to right (taking care not to damage the dove tail of the block); mark the new blade to correspond with the mark on the old, drive it in and adjust so that the mark coincides with the edge of the block. The blades will be adjusted by using the Clamp of tools foresight in the following manner:

Turn the screws of the clamp back, and place the clamp on the barrel so that the foresight block is between the gap of the clamp. Turn one of the screws up to the side of the foresight it is desired to press, and move the blade to the desired position. Remove the clamp, and replace the nose–cap and screws. When the correct position of the blade has been determined, the centre-punch will be used to fix it in position. A quarter turn of the screw of the No. 1, Mk. I Clamp =.01 inch—*i.e.*, approximately 2 inches on the target for each 100 yards range. Each division of the scale on the No. 1, Mk. I* and Mk. II Clamps = 4 inches on the target for the same range.

16. *Instructions for correcting the sighting of rifles in R.A.O.C. workshops when barrel with body is exchanged.*— After being fitted with a new barrel and body, the rifle will be tested by being fired on a 100-feet range. Sighting shots will be fired, and the foresight adjusted for lateral deviation, or replaced by another foresight to correct vertical deviation as necessary. The extent of the adjustment of the foresight in the block will be limited by the width of the block, i.e., neither side of the foresight must be within the corresponding side of the block, but may be flush with the block. If this limit of adjustment does not meet the case, the rifle will be examined for alignment of barrel in fore-end and nose-cap, and corrected as necessary. After correction of stocking, the rifle will again be tested.

17. Each rifle must invariably be used with the breech bolt bearing the rifle number, otherwise the lugs may not bear evenly, and the rifle may fire to the right or left; the distance from the bolt to the end of the chamber may also be affected. When, owing to loss or damage, it becomes necessary to fit another bolt to a rifle, the rifle should be fired for accuracy on the range. The fore-end and nose-cap are also fitted and numbered to the rifle. Accuracy tests must always be carried out when either or both of these components are exchanged.

18. When spare bolts, sight leaves, fore-ends and nose-caps are fitted

to rifles, they will be marked with the body number. When fitting a spare barrel with body, the whole of the components before mentioned will be re-marked with the new body number.

19. *Long-range sights.*—Action to be taken when details become unserviceable. In consequence of the abolition of long-range sights for Rifles, Nos. 1 and 2, unserviceable components of such sights will not be replaced, and action will be taken as follows: —

(i) If the bead, the pointer, the spring, or the pivot screw of the dial sight becomes unserviceable, the whole of these components will be removed and returned to store, the dial plate and fixing screw being left on the rifle for the purpose of covering the hole and recess in the fore-end. The aperture sight will be left on the rifle.

(ii) If either the dial plate or the fixing screw becomes unserviceable, the whole of the dial sight components will be removed and returned to store; the hole in the fore-end will be plugged with wood, the plug to be glued in.

(iii) If the aperture sight becomes unserviceable, the pillar will be filed off at the base and the base disc used as a washer under the spring. In case of deficiency, the washer, spring, bolt, locking, No. 1" will be employed to replace the aperture sight.

(iv) *Repair of rifles No. 1 D.P.*—Provision of stocks and handguards is made for the repair and maintenance of No. 1 D.P. (Drill Pupose) rifles. They are supplied, as required, on demand through the usual channels. These components, marked "D.P.", will not be used for the repair of rifles other than "D.P.". Serviceable stocks and handguards must not be used for the repair and maintenance of "D. P." rifles. Unserviceable stocks and handguards from service rifles which may be considered as suitable for "D.P." rifles will be accumulated locally at Command Ordnance Depots and held pending the visit of an examiner from the C.I.S.A., Enfield Lock, who will finally sentence and mark them. Serviceable components, other than stocks and handguards, may continue to be used for the maintenance of "D.P."

rifles provided that the cost is unlikely to exceed the cost of factory repair with "D.P." parts plus cost of transport of the rifles to and from the Royal Small Arms Factory, Enfield Lock.

Rifles No. 3, Mk. I* (T) fitted with Telescopic Sight
Rifles No. 3, Mk. I* (F) fitted with Fine-adjustment Backsight

1. In case of misfires, the mainspring should be weighed from the cocking-piece with the trigger tester, and the protrusion of the striker, from the face of the bolt, and the radius of the point should be gauged. The mainspring cannot be weighed with the bolt closed, but only when the latter is drawn to the rear against the bolt stop. The cocking-piece should then be turned into the long cam way of the bolt, and the weight of the mainspring tested by applying the trigger tester against the stripping nib of the cocking-piece. To record the weight in the fully cocked position, the cocking-piece should be drawn back until the rear face is approximately 5/8 inch in rear of the rear end of the bolt plug. Misfires are liable to be caused by an accumulation of oil in the spring chamber of the bolt, or at the cocking-piece seating in the bolt plug. These parts of the action should be kept free from heavy oil, mineral jelly, and dirt.

2. *Weights of springs.*—The springs can be tested with the trigger tester and should weigh as follows: —
Pull-off, from 5 lb. to 6 lb.
Pull to move trigger, from. 2 lb. to 3 lb.
Pull to move extractor (about) 4 lb.
Pull to lift butt trap by the nib (about) 2 ½ lb.
Pull to move bolt stop, from 2½ lb. to 4 lb.
Weight of mainspring from cocking-piece with spring eased from 8 lb. to 10 lb.
Weight at full cock from 13 lb. to 15 lb.

3. *Extraction.*—The extracting cam in the body and on the bolt should withdraw the bolt from .08-inch to .10-inch. Failure to extract may be due to a defective cartridge, or to the hook or retaining nib of the extractor being broken.

4. *Ejection.*—In the case of faulty ejection, test the ejector for freedom of movement with the bolt in the position it would be at the moment of ejection. The ejector should be quite free when upward or downward pressure is applied to the bolt lever, and should not friction in the slot in the bolt lug. If ejection is unsatisfactory, remove the ejector and test its straightness, as a bent ejector will friction in the slot of the bolt. Remove any thick grease, grit, particles of brass, etc., if present in the ejector slot in body and bolt.

5. *Fitting striker.*—In fitting a new striker, care must be taken to adjust it to length; the gauge, striker point No. 2 is provided for this purpose. There is also a similar gauge on the side of the implement, action No. 2. The striker should also be carefully rounded to the radius in the gauge or implement. A long or badly-rounded striker is likely to cause pierced caps. Before finally assembling the striker in the bolt, the striker should be inserted separately (*i.e.*, without bolt plug, etc.). The protrusion of the point should then be excessive, thus ensuring that, when assembled, the collar of the striker is not bearing at the bottom of the spring chamber. The forward position of the striker is determined by the cocking-piece seating in the bolt plug; the nose of the cocking- piece should not bear against the front end of the long cam. If the protrusion is insufficient, the front face of the cylindrical portion of the cocking-piece should be slightly adjusted by an oilstone until the correct protrusion is obtained.

5. *Fitting sear.*—When fitting a new sear, the height of the stud should be so regulated as to prevent the trigger from functioning correctly until the bolt is fully closed. (A low stud will permit of the sear releasing the cocking-piece with the bolt lever partially raised.)

7. *To correct or adjust "double pull."*—At the top or crown of the trigger, two radial nibs are formed— "A" and "B" (*see* drawing S.A.I.D. 2059)—the first pull is obtained by the leverage of the front nib "A"

against the underside of the body. On continuing to press the trigger rearwards, its movement is checked by the rear of nib "B" coming into contact with the seating at the underside of the body. Therefore, if the "1st pull" is too long, the height of the front nib "A" should be reduced with an oilstone, care being taken to maintain the correct shape. If the "1st pull" is short, it indicates that the rear nib "B" is too high, and should be reduced. A short "2nd pull" or "hair trigger" is a source of danger, and is not permissible. The bent of the sear, and also of the cocking-piece, should be perfectly square and vertical, and not inclined; these faces must not receive adjustment during the regulation of the "pull off." If the weights of the "pull-off": are light, the sear spring should be replaced by a stronger one.

8. *Fitting locking bolt.*—After inserting a new locking bolt, see that the front end does not protrude into the bolt lever way sufficiently to friction against the bolt lever.

9. *Extractor.*—When fitting a new extractor, see that the outside of the leg is not bowed excessively, since, if so, it is liable to friction in the body during withdrawal of the bolt, thereby causing the cartridge-case to be released from the bolt face recess, and resulting in faulty ejection.

10. *Catch, magazine.*—If it is found necessary to adjust the length when fitting a new catch, care should be taken to maintain the bevel at the front end, as this is essential to ensure retention of the bottom plate in case of a jolt or blow.

11. *To fit new stock.*—Remove from the old stock the following components :— Dial sight assembled, fixing screw and washer; stop band pin; collars, front and rear; tie nut and bolt; screws and bracket, with swivel, butt plate with screws. Assemble such of these components as are required to the new stock; then place the nose-cap on the stock and insert the front end of the handguard; if necessary,

plane or file the upper surfaces of the stock until the handguard fits the nose- cap and lies evenly on the stock. Place the action in the stock, with the rear handguard retaining ring placed in its correct position; if necessary, adjust the ring seating in the stock to ensure that the ring is not subjected to excessive stress when the action is screwed down securely, and, if required, plane or file the upper surfaces of the stock until the rear handguard fits in the ring and lies evenly on the surfaces.

The rear face of the transverse rib on the underside of the body should bear definitely against its seating; in order to ensure this, the stock should be cleared if necessary to prevent the rear end of the body tang from bearing at the end of the tang recess. The underside and front and rear ends of the body, and the reinforce of the barrel, should bear definitely in the stock. The barrel at the muzzle end should bear lightly against the stock when the body and reinforce bearings have been correctly adjusted. There should be sufficient clearance in the barrel groove between the reinforce and nose-cap seating to allow a piece of thick brown paper to be passed round and drawn along the barrel.

The length of the guard screw collars should be adjusted so that the trigger guard is tightened against the face of the collar and also the stock. See that the bolt lever is not prevented by the stock from closing fully down, as this may cause the locking bolt to remain jammed, owing to the recess in the rear face of the bolt lever not being in alignment with the locking bolt. See also that the bolt stop is not prevented, by fullness of the stock, from closing freely.

Before assembling, finally grease the barrel groove of the stock and handguards, and also the barrel and body, with red mineral jelly.

12. *Exchanging bolt.*—When fitting new bolts, the distance of the bolt from the end of the chamber should be tested with the gauges

—.064-inch No. 2, and .074-inch No. 2 to ensure that neither too much, nor too little, space exists between these two points. The locking lugs must not be oil-stoned or otherwise adjusted to enable the bolt to close over the .064-inch gauge; selection of a bolt that will fit the rifle is the only permissible procedure.

13. *Adjustment of foresight.*—The method of adjusting the foresight laterally is similar to that for rifles No. 1, except that the No. 2 cramp will be used for the purpose.

Sight-Telescopic
Rifles No. 3, Mk. I* (T)
(With leather caps and strap, and case with leather sling and cap, cleaning cloth, wire brush, and eye guard).

General Information
Description and Method of
Adjustment

The telescopic sight is specially adjusted and numbered, before issue, to the rifle to which it is fitted, and forms part of the rifle with which it must always be kept. Whenever adjustment is necessary beyond that which armourers are allowed to carry out, the rifle complete with telescopic sight and the details mentioned in the heading should be forwarded to the C.I.S.A. in the chest provided. The sight is not issued separately. The case, sight, telescopic, with leather sling and cap, cleaning cloth and wire brush, and the eye-guard are issue-able separately for maintenance. The cleaning cloth and brush can also be supplied separately for maintenance.

The cloth is provided for cleaning the lenses, and the wire brush for keeping the fittings on the rifle free from dust; both are carried under the flap inside the cap of the case. The eye-guard is a conical rubber. Tube, 3 ½ inches long, beaded at one end and beveled at the other. The beaded end fits over the eye-guard body of the telescope. The two leather caps connected by the strap are provided for protecting the lenses; care should be taken to prevent oil from getting on to the lenses. When not in actual use, the telescope should be carried in the case.

Telescope.—The telescope consists of a steel body containing a combination of lenses. The two eye lenses are separated by a distance ring and secured by a locking ring. The erector has two lenses—a clamp ring, and cell-locking ring and stop. It is held by the focusing slide (1) and focusing slide clamping screw (2), on the underside of

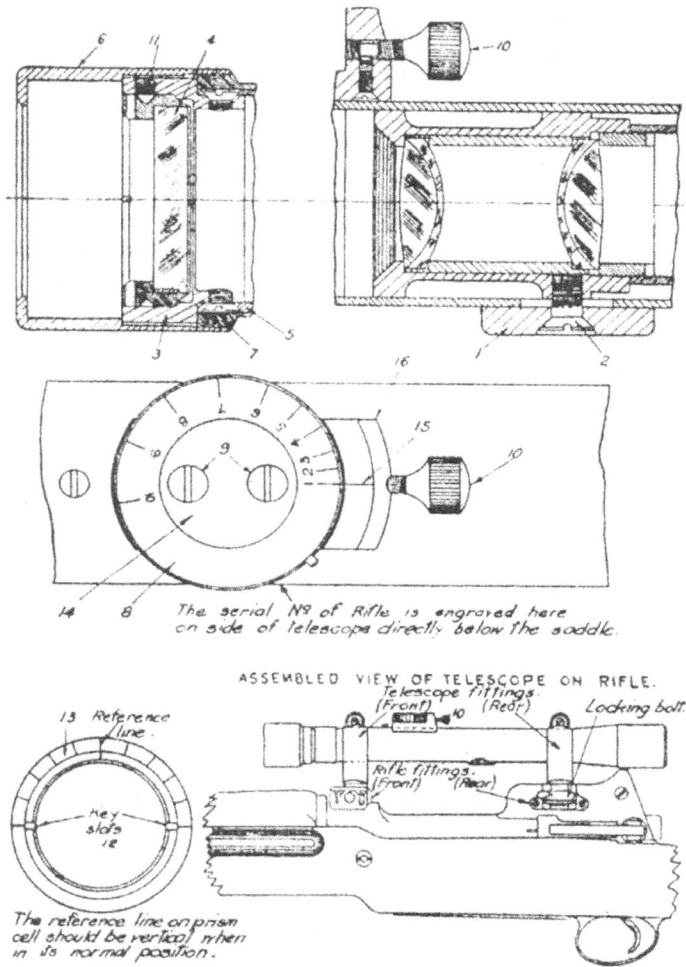

ASSEMBLED VIEW OF TELESCOPE ON RIFLE.

The serial Nº of Rifle is engraved here on side of telescope directly below the saddle.

The reference line on prism cell should be vertical when in its normal position.

Fig. 8.

the body. The object glass is held in a sleeve screwed into the front

Adjustments

The only adjustments to the telescopic sights of rifles which may be

attempted by armourers attached to units are:
The alteration for lateral deflection by means of the prism. The adjustment of focus, zeroing and setting of the range scale. The interior or other parts of the instrument must not be touched.

Lateral adjustment.—Lateral adjustment is effected by means of a glass wedge or prism (4) mounted in front of the object glass. This prism deflects a ray of light passing through it towards its thicker end. If, therefore, the prism is mounted with its thicker edge on top and horizontal, and the rifle to which the telescopes fitted is laid in rests, so that the bull's-eye of a distant target is found upon the tip of the pointer, then a complete rotation of the prism about the axis of the telescope, in a clockwise direction, as seen from the eye-piece of the telescope, will cause the image of the bull's-eye in the plane of the diaphragm to rotate in a small circle passing, say, from 12 o'clock through 3, 6 and 9 o'clock, back to 12 o'clock.

Thus, when the thick end of the prism is horizontal, the image will be positioned either at 12 or 6 o'clock, and the displacement of it, for any small angular displacement of the prism, will be practically horizontal duly.

This fact is taken advantage of for the purpose of securing adjustment for lateral deflection. The prism is initially mounted as nearly as possible with its thick edge horizontal, so that any required small adjustment for deflection can be effected without materially affecting the adjustment for elevation.
Note.—*The prism is in the form of a circular disc, but in this paragraph it is spoken of as though left in its primitive shape of a square.*

Method of adjustment.—Remove ray shade (6). Slacken the three screws fixing prism cell (11), fit the adjusting key into the slots of the prism cell (12), and rotate to the right or left as necessary. There is a reference line on the ring of the prism cell adaptor (13). If the prism cell is rotated through one of these divisions, it will give approximately five minutes of deflection.

When correct adjustment has been made, tighten up the screws fixing prism cell (11) and replace the ray shade (6).

Adjustment for elevation.—The drum head of the elevating screw is fitted with a movable range scale ring (8) upon which the range scale is engraved. This ring is normally secured by a washer (14) and two fixing screws (9) to the drum head of the elevating screw. If at any time it is found that the elevation indicated by the scale is wrong for any given range, it can be put right by unclamping the range scale ring, adjusting the pointer by shooting at a known range, and then turning the range scale ring to indicate this range before clamping it once more to the drum head of the elevating screw.

Order of adjustment.—It is important to note that when ever an adjustment for lateral deflection by rotation of the prism has been made, the accuracy of the range scale for elevation should be checked, as it may happen that the initial position of the prism was not one in which its thick edge was perfectly horizontal. In adjusting the telescope, therefore, it is important that the adjustment for lateral deflection should be made first; then, if necessary, the adjustment for elevation should be made. Should the adjustment for elevation be made first, it may happen that the subsequent adjustment for deflection introduces an error in the adjustment for elevation.

To adjust focus.—Remove the telescope from the rifle, release the screw, clamping, focusing slide (2) and adjust the slide (1) to suit the eye, tighten the screw and replace the telescope on the rifle.

To adjust for zero after shooting at 200-yards.—Release the screws fixing washer scale ring (9) and turn the range scale ring until the second line corresponds with the zero line (15) on the saddle

(16), then re-tighten the screws fixing washer (9). Clamp the drum with the screw clamping range drum (10) after shooting for zero at 200 yards or adjusting for other ranges.

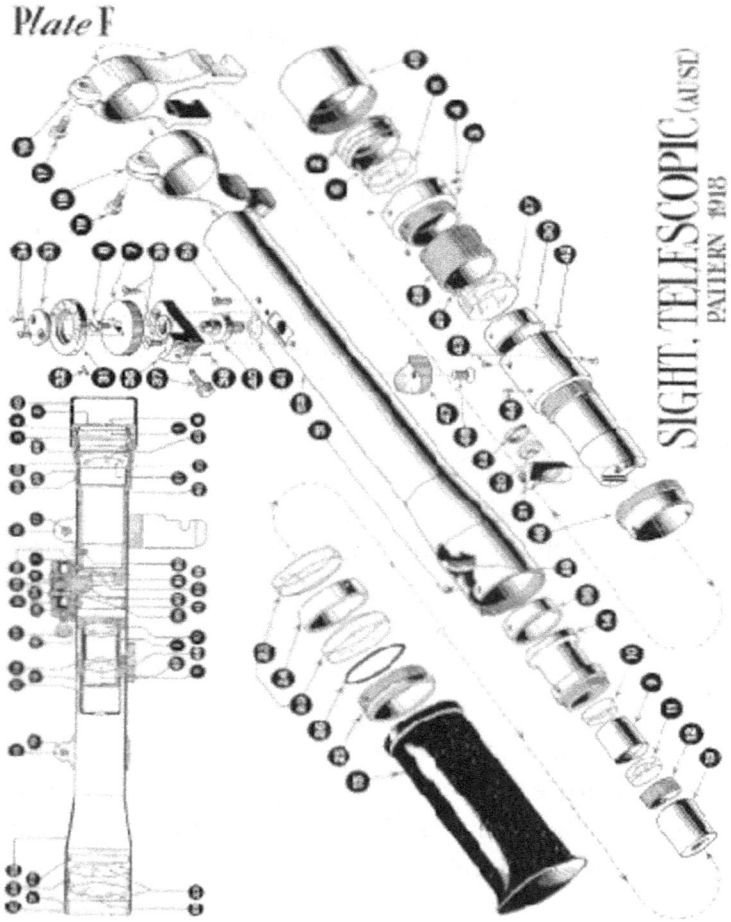

Plate F

SIGHT, TELESCOPIC (AUST) PATTERN 1918

Packing of telescopic sights during storage.—In order to prevent the formation of verdigris on the brass caps, etc., of the sights during storage, the leather caps will not be placed on the sight, but will be inserted separately in the case. The steel body tube and brackets of the sight will be cleaned with an oily rag and wiped quite dry; the telescope will then be wrapped in plain, dry tissue paper before insertion in the case. Care must be taken to see that the tissue paper used is perfectly dry. The case will be stored in the chest with the rifle.

Tools.—The following tools are provided for the adjustment of telescopic sights: — Key, sight, telescopic.

Screwdrivers, Instrument makers (set of 4).
The above-mentioned tools will form part of the "Box, tool, regimental armourers" in peace, and of the "Bag, armourers, S.A." in war, for units equipped with telescopic- sighted rifles.

SECTION 5.

Re-browning and Re-blacking

1. For general instructions, assistance to be provided by units, etc., *see* Part I, Chapter III, and Appendix I. The following components of rifles will be re-browned when required

Rifles Nos. 1 *and* 2. —Barrel with foresight block, inner band and backsight bed; body; bolt; bolt-head; cocking- piece; locking bolt and spring; trigger guard; magazine; outer band; handguard cap; backsight protector; nose-cap; backsight cap (or windgauge) and swivel bracket. Also cut-off of No. I, Mk. III rifles.

Rifles No. 3, Mk.I* (T) and Mk. I* (F).—Parts of a corresponding nature to those for Nos. 1 and 2 rifles. As these rifles are provided only for sniping purposes, re-browning will seldom be necessary.

The rifles are specially tested and adjusted for accuracy before issue from the factory; care must therefore be taken to keep the parts separate from those of other rifles; they should be stripped only when actually necessary for purposes of re-browning, oiling, and minor adjustment or repair.

2. When cleaning off the surplus browning from the frictional surfaces of bolts and bolt-heads and the bolt hole of bodies, care must be taken to avoid the use of sharp abrasives; it is essential that the size of these parts should be maintained as long as possible.

Oil-blacking
    1. Oil-blacking will be limited to foresight blades, swivels, and

screws. As fore sight blades are hardened and tempered, the temperature should not be raised above the minimum required for oil-blacking.

2. It should be borne in mind that certain other hardened and tempered parts, *e.g.*, cocking-pieces, locking bolts, cut-offs, etc., which are oil-blacked in factories, are subjected to special treatment and inspection tests which it is not possible for armourers to repeat; when such parts are worn bright, they should be browned.

Temporary Blacking of Sights and other Parts

For the temporary blacking of sights and other parts which are worn bright only at some local point, and which do not require complete treatment by browning, the following process will be found suitable:—

Dissolve 1 oz. of liver shellac in 6 oz. of methylated spirits and add to the mixture as much "carbon black" (lamp black) as will fill six empty .303-inch cartridge-cases. The carbon black may be obtained by placing a piece of sheet iron over a gas jet, candle, or lamp flame. Thoroughly free the bright place to be blacked from oil, and coat lightly with the above mixture, using a camel-hair brush. Care must be taken to keep the mixture securely corked up, otherwise it will evaporate quickly.

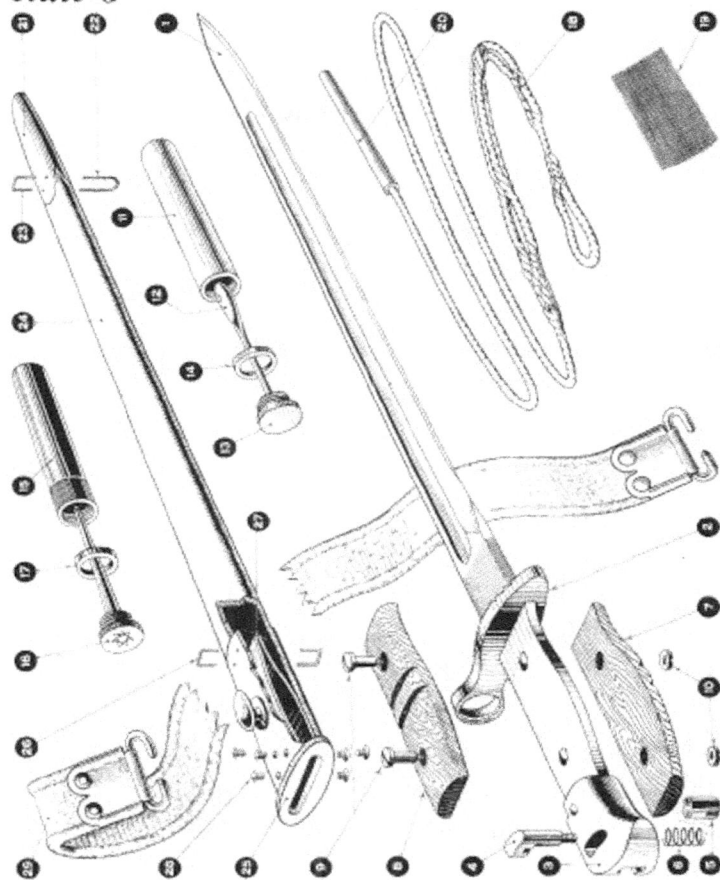

Plate G

SECTION 6.

Description and Use of Armourers' Gauges
and certain Tools and Gauges

Gauges, armourers', .064-inch No 1 and .074-inch No. 1 for rifles No.1. -These gauges are used also for .303-inch machine- guns, with the exception of the .074, which is not used for Vickers guns.

The gauges are for testing the distance of the face of the breech bolt from the end of the chamber, or, in other words, the cartridge head space. The diameter of the rim conforms approximately to that of a maximum cartridge. The portion which enters the chamber is merely a guide—not a gauging feature.

When closing the bolt on the gauge, the trigger should be held back to prevent cocking and snapping, which is liable to cause the rim of the gauge to be broken off. Care should also be taken to avoid drawing the gauge back on to, and so damaging, the ejector. In no circumstances must these gauges be used for No. 3 rifles, as the rim is slightly too large in diameter for the recess in the face of the bolt of those rifles, and, consequently, in addition to giving a false gauging result, will cause damage to the wall of the recess or the projecting horns on the left recoil lug of the bolt.

Gauges, armourers', .064-inch No.2 and .074-inch No.2 for rifles No 3.— These gauges are special to No. 3 rifles and must be used only for those rifles. They differ from the No. 1 gauges in that the diameter of the rim is smaller and the portion which enters the chamber is longer, the front end being tapered off.

The instructions given for the use of the No. 1 gauges are applicable also to the No. 2 gauges.

The No. 2 gauges are obtainable on loan from store when required.

Gauges, armourers' plug—.303,.307,.308, .310,*and lead No. 2 with rod, plug Mk. II.*—These gauges are held in R.A.O.C. Ordnance depots and are supplied to circuit armourers at home and abroad when required. The .303 gauge is supplied to all armourers. At stations abroad, the gauges may also be issued on loan to regimental armourers when the services of a circuit armourer are not available.

The plugs are screwed internally at the rear end to take the rod. The . 307, .308, .310 and lead are limit gauges for wear of bore of .303-inch rifle barrels—*see* Section 3.

The .308 plug has a line marked round it at ¼ inch from the front end, the limit being reached when this line is flush with the muzzle of the barrel.

The .310 and lead plugs are arranged so that the limit in rifles No. 1 is reached when the rear end of either plug is flush with, or inside, the breech face of the barrel, the distance from the line marked- round the .310 plug to the front end of the plug is the same as the distance from the breech face to the front end of the lead, but as the diameter of the bore and of the front portion of the lead, in new or part worn barrels, is less than .310 inch, the line will stand out from the breech face of such barrels for a distance which will diminish as wear increases.

In the case of No. 3 rifles, the limit is reached with the .310 plug when the line on the rod, one inch from the face of the collar, is flush with, or inside, the rear face of the front socket portion of the body; with the No. 2 lead plug the limit is reached when the line 1 ¼ inch from the face of the collar so enters.

The lines referred to are ¼ and ½ inch further from the face of the collar than the M.G. line for machine guns in naval service.

When Mk. I rods, plug, are in possession, and are required for use in gauging No. 3 rifles, they will be altered to Mk. II pattern by armourers by the marking of the two additional lines referred to.

Gauges, armourers', striker point No.1 for rifles Nos.1 and 2. —The dimensions for striker protrusion through the face of the bolt-head are .042 inch high and .04 inch low, and the radius of the point .038 inch.

Gauges, armourers', striker point No.2 for rifles No.3.—The dimensions for striker protrusion in this gauge are .055 inch high and .05 inch low, and the radius of point .03 inch. This gauge is supplied on loan as required.

Tester, trigger.—This is provided for testing the weight or tension of the various rifle springs and pull-off referred to in Sections 3 and 4, and for pistols, Chapter III. It can be used also for machine-guns when the spring balance provided for use with those guns is not available.

In order to obtain a correct result, it is essential that those working parts of the weapons which are either directly or indirectly linked up with the springs should be thoroughly clean; when dried oil, mineral jelly or other matter is present, a true reading will not be obtained.

When testing the pull-off of a rifle, the rifle should be, if possible, gripped firmly in a horizontal position in a vice, cut-off side uppermost, the tester then being applied diagonally across the small of the butt in the line taken by the normal finger-pull.

When testing Nos. 1 and 2 rifles, fitted with the No. 1 "B" cocking-piece, for weight of mainspring in both spring- eased and full-cock positions, apply the hook of the tester either in the half-bent or locking bolt recess at the side of the cocking-piece. In order to do this, it is necessary to with-draw the bolt and turn the cocking-piece into the long cam of the bolt, first marking the striker lightly to indicate the full cock position.

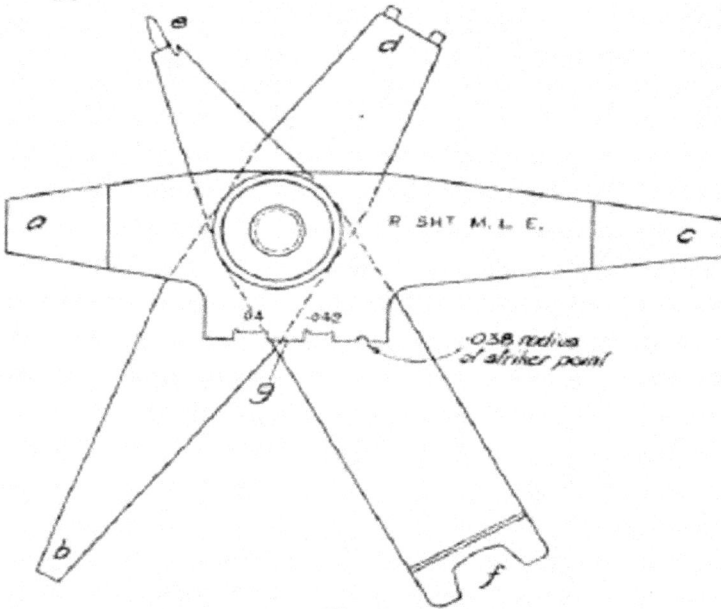

Fig. 9.

Reference gauges and tester, trigger.—A list of these gauges is given in E.R., Pt. I. The gauges are kept at Ordnance depots where armourers shops are established; they are to be employed solely for the periodical verification of the working gauges, and must not on any account be used as working gauges.

The working gauges will be tested for comparison with the reference gauges as follows: —

Gauges .064 No. 1 and .074 No. 1. —Select No. 1 rifles in which the bolt just closes over the working gauge, then apply the reference gauge.

Gauges, plug.—Select barrels which are worn to the limits according to the working gauges, then apply the reference gauges.

In the case of the .303-inch plug, select a barrel in which the working gauge runs and is a fit, and then apply the reference gauge, bearing in mind that a very small difference, *e.g.*, .0001 inch in the gauges will admit of the smaller entering and the larger being kept out. The .303 gauge, not being a limit gauge, can be allowed to wear to a greater extent than the limit gauges. .3025 is a reasonable limit.

Tester, trigger.—Select a rifle in which the first pull and the pull-off are to the minimum weights with the working tester, then apply the reference tester. When a marked difference from the reference gauges is found, *i.e.*, if the rifles would undoubtedly be sentenced for exchange with the working gauges or testers, but not so with the reference gauges or tester, a report should be made, and the worn working gauges returned to store for exchange. Similar action should be taken when wear of the .064 working gauge is such that there is a possibility of rifles, when tested with the gauges, failing to turn over a cartridge with rim of maximum thickness without undue pressure on the bolt handle.

Tools

Implement action No. 1, Mk. II.—The various tools and the gauge comprising the implement (*see* Fig. 9 above) are provided for the following purposes

(*a*) Screwdriver for the following screws: — inner band, nose-cap (back), trigger guard (front), butt-plate, locking bolt spring and backsight protector nut.

(*b*) Screwdriver for cut-off, extractor & handguard cap screws.

(*c*) Screwdriver for the following, screws: — outer band, swivels, marking disc, ejector, trigger guard (back), sear, backsight spring and windgauge.

(*d*) Screwdriver for backsight slide catch screw.

(*e*) Tool for removing and replacing extractor spring.

(*f*) Screwdriver for bolt nut of bayonets.

(*g*) Gauge for projection and radius of striker point (dimensions as for gauge striker point No. 1).

Tools, breeching up.—These tools are now issued only, as ordered, to India and Dominions overseas, but those which may still be available at Command workshops and at Weedon will continue to be used for un-breeching unserviceable barrels from serviceable bodies prior to breaking up the barrels.

Plates, screw and taps S.A.—Particulars of these plates and taps, and the screws, etc., for which they are suitable are given.

Thread Sizes

Rifle No 1 Mark III & III*			
Screw, cap, nose, front	B15	.1875 dia x 33 tpi	Later examples have larger head and wider slot.
Screw, extractor retaining	A45	.126 dia x 42 tpi	
Striker	A49	.25 dia x 30 tpi	Whitworth form?
Screw, striker retaining	A50	.144 dia x 37t pi	Two types: - Domed, wide slot - Flat head, narrow slot.
Screw, guard, trigger, back	B27	.144 dia x 37 tpi	Also longer version for attaching aperture sights. Commercial sources.
Screw, cap, nose, back	B14	.1875 dia x 33 tpi	
Screw, piling swivel	B17	.1875 dia x 33 tpi	
Screw, butt-trap spring	B49	.1656 dia x 37 tpi	
Screw, cap, handguard, front	B20	.096 dia x 56 tpi	
Screw, bayonet grip	C09	.1656 dia x 37tpi	Later spares use 3BA
Screw, backsight protector	B33	.1875 dia x 33 tpi	Counter sunk m/c screw
Screw, cut-off	A36	.114 dia x 49 tpi	All marks bar Mark III*
Screw, trigger guard, front	B28	.25 dia x 30 tpi	
Screw, outer band	B11	.1875 dia x 33 tpi	
Screw Windage Backsight No1	N/A	.17 dia x 46 dia	On Mk III only and some re-worked III*.
Screw, sear	A39	.1745 dia x 50 tpi	
Screw, ejector	A37	.1656 dia x 37 tpi	2 lengths - .205 (obsolescent), .23 current
Screw, catch,slide,backsight	A20	.1875 dia x 33 tpi	
Bolt Bayonet Patt 1907	C4	.181 dia x 26-1/3tpi	
Screw, dial sight fixing	NA	.181 dia x 26-1/3 tpi	Different for P14

Screw, sling swivel rear	B43	.1875 dia x 33 tpi	
Bolt, Stock	B36	7/16" BSW (14tpi)	
Bolt Head	A47	.4175 dia x 20 tpi	75-78deg, incl flank angle. Enfield form.
Screw, cap, backsght	A13	.1656 dia x 37 tpi	
Screw, back sight spring	A25	.144 dia x 37 tpi	
Screw, inner band	A03	.1875 dia x 33 tpi	
Screw, safety catch spring	A33	.1656 dia x 37 tpi	

Rifle No 3 (Pattern 14)

Screw, axis	D09	.096 dia x 56 tpi	1.18 o/all length
Screw, nose cap	C05	.1656 dia x 37 tpi	
Screw, axis, backsight	A07	.096 dia x 56 tpi	
Screw, stop backsight	A13	.084 dia x 57 tpi	
Screw, backsight spring	A15	.144 dia x 37 tpi	
Screw, catch bolt locking	B05	.12 dia x 48 tpi*	
Screw, axis	B14	.126 dia x 42 tpi	
Screw, front band	C03	.1875 dia x 33 tpi	Common to SMLE
Screw, dial sight fixing	C30	.1656 dia x 37 tpi	Different to SMLE
Screw, piling swivel	C07	.1875 dia x 33 tpi	
Screw, back, trigger guard	C15	.25 dia x 30 tpi	
Screw, front, trigger guard	C16	.25 dia x 30 tpi	
Screw, volley dial sight	C30	.1656 dia x 37 tpi	

Screw, fine adjustment.	D07	.088 dia x 36 tpi*	
Screw, stop sight	D15	.084 dia x 57 tpi	
Screw, back sight leaf	D17	.144 dia x 37 tpi	2.0 o/all length
Screw, catch bolt locking	D22	.12 dia x 48 tpi*	As per B5
Screw, butt-trap spring	C38	.1656 dia x 37 tpi	

www.ingramcontent.com/pod-product-compliance
Lightning Source LLC
Chambersburg PA
CBHW071633040426
42452CB00009B/1605